Chuck Whelon

DOVER PUBLICATIONS, INC.
Mineola, New York

Note

This unique book takes dozens of almost-finished pictures about Christmas and invites you, the reader, to complete them! You'll have a chance to decorate Christmas stockings, add an ornament to a branch, show some ice skaters on a frozen pond, and even draw a scene in a snow globe. Grab a pencil and get ready to do some Christmas drawing!

Copyright

Copyright © 2011 by Dover Publications, Inc.
All rights reserved..

Bibliographical Note

What to Doodle? Christmas Creations! is a new work, first published by Dover Publications, Inc., in 2011.

International Standard Book Number

ISBN-13: 978-0-486-48530-0
ISBN-10: 0-486-48530-7

Manufactured in the United States by Courier Corporation
48530702
www.doverpublications.com

Draw some presents around this Christmas tree.

Who's going to open these presents?

Draw some of the inhabitants of the Candy Cane Forest.

Where are Santa and his reindeer flying off to, and what kind of weather are they having?

Draw the toy that this elf is working on in Santa's Workshop.

Build a friend for this snowman.

Decorate these Christmas stockings.

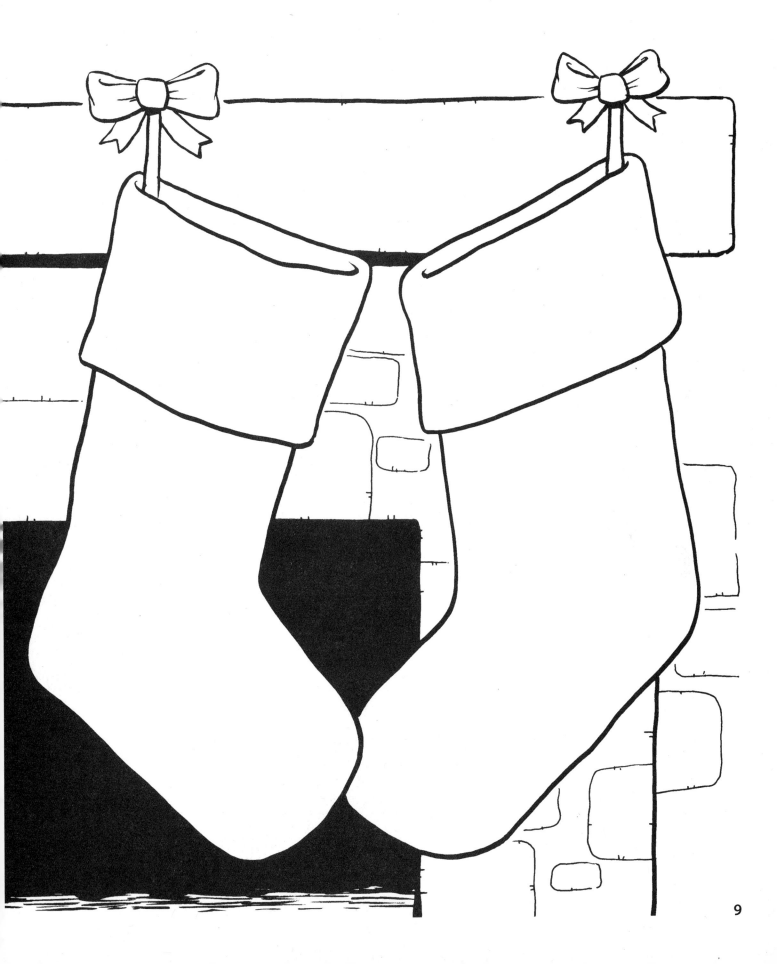

9

Draw a silly hat for this silly elf.

Who are the carolers singing to?

What Christmas present did kitty get this year?

Draw a candle to complete this dinner-table centerpiece.

Draw a special ornament to hang on the Christmas tree branch.

Draw the gift you'd most like to get this Christmas.

Decorate these holiday cookies.

17

Draw a nice warm fire in this fireplace.

Design a Christmas card to send to your friends and family.

What gift will you give your best friend this Christmas?

Draw a decorative Christmas wreath on this front door.

Draw some crazy Christmas decorations in this front yard.

Little Betty's snowman just came to life—can you draw it?

Decorate the wrapping paper on these gifts.

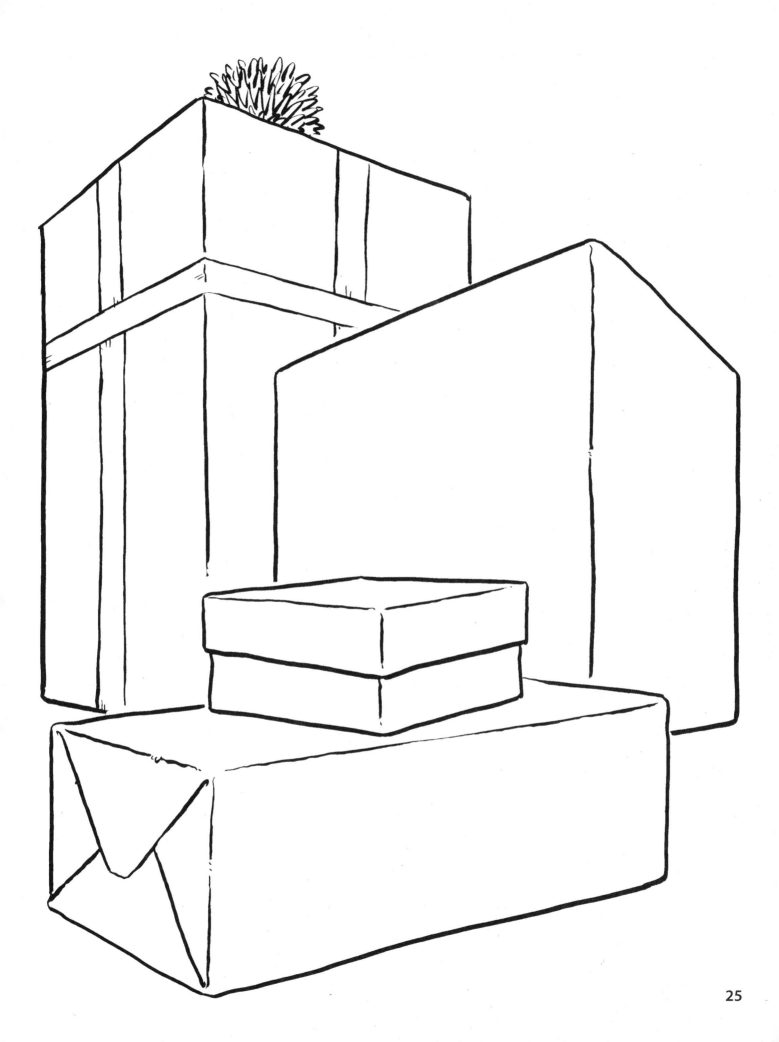

Draw a gingerbread house for this gingerbread family.

What's in this pear tree?

Oh, no! What mean, Christmas-hating creature has stolen this girl's toys?

Put some Christmas lights all over this house.

Draw some of the creatures you might see in this snowy landscape.

Draw some Christmas decorations to brighten up this room.

What has Santa got in his sack?

Who is about to kiss under this mistletoe?

Draw a dancing partner for the Nutcracker.

Welcome to the North Pole! Can you draw some of its inhabitants?

Decorate this gingerbread man.

What has this boy found in his Christmas pudding?

The lake has frozen over—draw some people having fun on the ice!

41

'Tis the night before Christmas—and who is stirring in this house?

Who left these footprints on the roof?

Draw a spectacular stage design for these holiday dancers.

Draw a beard for Santa.

Who has come to visit mean old Scrooge on Christmas Eve?

Decorate this yule log with a miniature festive scene.

Draw the hottest-selling item that all the Christmas shoppers are struggling to get.

What is Tiny Tim going to have for Christmas dinner?

Who's going on this sleigh ride together?

It's always Christmas in a snow globe! What scene will you put in this one?

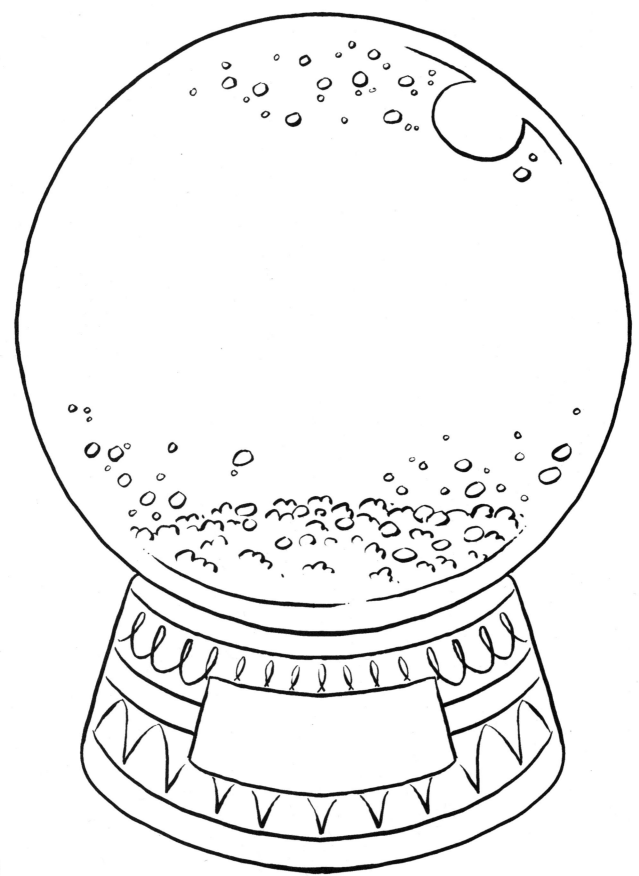

Draw some antlers for this reindeer.

Can you draw some more snowflakes? Remember that no two are ever alike!

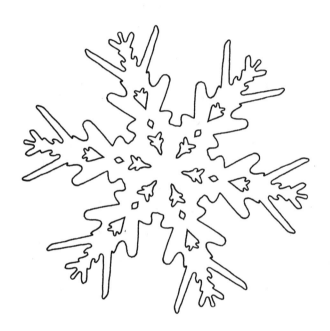

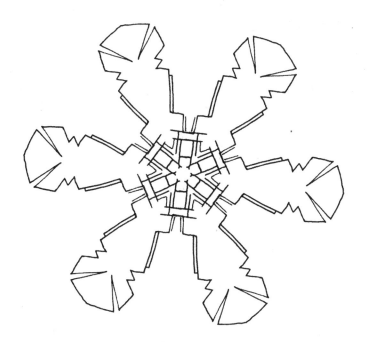

What treats will you leave out for Santa?

Christmas is often a time for travel. Where would you like to visit this year?

In Australia, December 25th is in the middle of summer—how would you celebrate Christmas on the beach?

What is this Christmas star shining over?